DISSUASION CROWDS THE SLOW WORKER

LORI LUBESKI

O Books

For Karen

I.

Having missed the
train in fragments

                              words bring out
                              the idea of the lost feeling
                              never can adequately say
                              what is down there

Ghosts in one's own yard
the smell of garlic

that I would not ever to that degree again be cold

  .

until beyond six
you work still
I contemplate your noise
in the back room
train arises
you sudden jump on
we would not care for coffee
or no even tea

                              someone smoking provokes
                              the idea of you having been
                              here before

in a low half note
silent blessing, or miracle

your words profile
the edge of any possibility

.

a man exits and a boy enters
how many more childhoods we must reorganize
due to bad or cliff dreams
swimming bloody faces the wave
hits you, your color drains

                                    not even contemplating
                                    the force of your body
                                    being slapped against the rock

instead you clean up after
a man staying in your grandfather's house
him dying, not being able to
tell the man to go,
being dirty, I sweep the floor

                    .

                                    the boys diving
                                    from high cliffs
                                    dramatize my desire

burning of indefinitely through the tunnel
a place you would never go
my ears listening for cues
to again start breathing

                                        a girl playing hopscotch
                                        falls down on her knee is scraped

boats with tall sails
men reading maps
you fall into another lifetime
lose track of the meaning

                        of Oakland City Center 12th Street

would not have foraged along
thus/this far without the desire
to be in the sand with the water breaking close
and the sun still winter

find ourselves
repeating exact feelings
of any other particular situation

                        .

                                        how corrupt the world is
                                        you view eating as a distraction
                                        in the same way
                                        as not to having thought

about the significance
of rearranging your childhood,
growing up

                    growing up not looking

here the colors blend otherwise

                        .

If the way several boys were talking
symbolized my ability
to be associated with a group at this time

                              you lean toward my direction
                              cold after your bath

                    in a body naked
                    and thinning from after heat
                    of water and the boys desiring you

                        .

Framework of a pattern
dislocating from its structure
and what one person
has learned
from another person

behind her glasses
a woman blinks
under disguised vision

                          a catastrophe destroys
                          all sense of balance
                          is similar to not eating

the way it distracts the boys from being silent

or having missed my stop
accidentally they exit here

your attachment to my blood
on your sheets
distracts you from eating
my absence and the inability
to do your laundry

                          A derailed freight train
                          in a boy's young childhood
                          creates the sensation of
                          not understanding

                          as in leaving a place alone
                          narrows the point of view

not to shock
or relay shocking news
to someone calmly resting
in the warm bath water

Displaced desire
attracts you to women
who make your lunch
walk you to the train station
the boy balancing memory
and attention as he concentrates on

                              a flashback
                              of a mother's reproductive system
                              living inside of fluid
                              breathing walls of organs

not the ability to do but depend

                              on a level of blood
                              waves pushing me up against
                              the rocks, my face

                              .

do babies realize
if someone else
has been in the womb
before them

is there a signal, a trace

of the vulnerability we experience when the shift in texture

being accustomed to
something and having
it removed

                                       your brother's stillness
                                       in contemplating the missing
                                       location of adolescence

as a catastrophe throws one's life
out of balance you wake with the burden
of every emotion you had missed
before the need to rearrange your childhood

                  emerges with the boys out of waves

                                .

                                         having been in another place
                                       boats with high windows
                                     cargo ships
                                     and the meaning of transferring
                                     at MacArthur Station

Going home early from work
you feel privileged
stops with people waiting for your body
boy's desire in chilled sheets my blood
on your white/skin we remove

a man's eyes focus mine on the sun
setting the way underprivileged people
do not take vacations or leave work early

what the woman sees behind her glasses

views I had thought would appear differently

.

The men's eyes
resemble our desire
to have that degree
of absent thought

to move quickly,

as in the end of a movie

the credits past your eyes

.

being accustomed to
something and having
it removed

                              your brother's stillness
                              in contemplating the missing
                              location of adolescence

as a catastrophe throws one's life
out of balance you wake with the burden
of every emotion you had missed
before the need to rearrange your childhood

            emerges with the boys out of waves

                    .

                              having been in another place
                              boats with high windows
                              cargo ships
                              and the meaning of transferring
                              at MacArthur Station

Going home early from work
you feel privileged
stops with people waiting for your body
boy's desire in chilled sheets my blood
on your white/skin we remove

a man's eyes focus mine on the sun
setting the way underprivileged people
do not take vacations or leave work early

what the woman sees behind her glasses

views I had thought would appear differently

.

The men's eyes
resemble our desire
to have that degree
of absent thought

to move quickly,

as in the end of a movie

the credits past your eyes

.

II.

Women carrying food
and disdain for those types
brings you further from
the approach of April

       the grass smell of your body after having walked
       through the park

                 parades of clowns
                 falter past your steps
                 out the window glows
                 ambulances

movement which resembles still
the sound of colored broth
in childhood memories

vending machines

                 total eclipse of sun
                 distorts your eyes
                 told not to look up
                 but having looked up anyway

the parade continually passing through an unused portion

           of your vision

          .

equipment carrying men
in trucks to places of employment
afterwards they go home
hungry the boys ask permission
from their fathers
to leave the house, the dinner table

play in used car lots
soup machines in body shops
colored broth of men wearing masks
to protect their faces

echoes

the garden, slow bleeding

forest of jazz intrusion
the sounds of your father
in rhythms beyond voice
a pull away

it comes on
you listen

the parade by your house yearly

subtracting from distance
the nearness of colors

in games on portions after the parade
clowns still on the sidewalk

.

being young we explore the train wreck
climb on the cars as if fascinated
our limbs swell in commotion
black of exhaust air participates

as tragedy passes
leaving your father's
voice playing over a record
on your stereo
you in my arms

boys appearing again
in the back of the train

in their desire a bland look on
your face resembling no trace of jazz
as children the tar of used car lots
prayers to the convenient saint

snow falls
home from school
6 hours later
it will have been winter
boats coming in
for the season

rowing ashore

your brother in his canoe we pretend to be Indians

III.

The grass smell of accidents
before the train would derail
next day stabbing a crowbar
through your foot
the meat coming out

                    your mother carrying you to the bathroom sink

not knowing your foot
would be in stitches
tomorrow you go to the train
wreck alone
thinking it was a planned event
in which no one was killed
supposed to be killed

                    the grass color in nightmares
                    20 years later duplicates
                    the smell of stitches
                    you are given a test drug
                    they see how far you stagger

before passing out your lover catches you in her arms
carries you to the place you will sleep

the poisoning sensation of
of women in Hitchcock films

                              nausea and its horrible
                              weakening effect

                    .

your mother bloodied
with your foot
her clean white nursing
uniform on her way to work

takes you to the doctor's
the boys and brothers leaning over you

                         .

you walk home alone from the crash
sky of nightmare's particular color
arrive at the house
of your mother and father

scenes that take place slowly

                              during being poisoned

IV.

Men carrying men
from places of wreckage

the slow whine or deliberation of engines

                    night with its maps
                    of the boy's desire
                    children to be playing
                    in used car lots

prayers to the suitable saint
in redeeming ourselves we act slowly
pause at intervals
follow you to the train stop
wait in front of opening doors
but don't get on

                    explore the emotions of having
                    been left

                         .

at the hardware store the boy dreams
you entering in thought the prayer
suffered died and was buried
resting calmly in the warm bath

                    him waiting

through misplaced childhood
in the opposite room
floor weighed down by footsteps

of my mother carrying me to the bathroom sink

to be dipped in water
your grandmother in the bath
with lemons and sour milk
to keep soft her skin

.

after the train wreck entered the papers
with a picture of the boy climbing
on the front page you see it reproduced
preserved image of yourself alone

the sharper the image
the further away it stays
from your belief
due to fear
in the subjunctive (conditional)

the boy in the hardware store
dating the prayer you have inside
your head feels alienated
instead you think of me

forgetting the prayer
through constant repetition
out of context the bleeding
disassociated from my body
has no appeal to you

on the way home the sky blackens, my father loses his
sister in a car accident as children he sees

               her falling down
               death of his mother
               repeats he goes inside
               not crying

my senses dull, the image becomes absent
in its clarity

the boy in the hardware store
waits for you
driving by we pass him on the sidewalk
his lungs in motion
signal

                        cold places seem less easily remembered

        .

leaving the train wreck alone
the need becomes disassembled
all constant forms gathered
in the description
of the pleasure given to you
by the boy in the hardware
store he feels alienated, us driving by

his job inconvenient

V.

An idea of   street arguments
close to your house
a man puts a women's head
through a window after having
dragged her across
public areas

                        as children you watch
                        look for constant motion
                        the fighting, the evergreens

consideration for
those who love you
your father's parents
buried in a cemetery
your brother visits
sees his name

white smooth otherwise loose print
        tragedy follows one so closely

                        in our exploration
                        of nearness

we learn to lean in the opposite direction

design of letters
etched on stone

.

breathing equivalent
to the slowness under the bridge
inside the tunnel

noise of speed
cement being travelled through

                        stillness, motion
                        blends

so that either one cannot be distinguished
                        from the other

sound of range
in our desire to be home

                    resting calmly in the warm bath water

.

the boy sleeps late
being on vacation
thinks of you dreaming
seeing you tomorrow
you point to him as we pass by

across my mother's white uniform

she returns home from work
with the gradual process of blood staining

the road jammed
with cars and other
people moving in
the direction
of someplace familiar

intersect at a given point

under the bridge something terrible
having happened
in order to rearrange your childhood

you drift from the measured feeling
a nervous throat drops
the death of a child
on Sunday the way a tragedy

indicates the absence of protection

feeling only 9 years old
on the train home today
a man listens to conversation
other than the one he is engaged in

the boy in the hardware store
sits in the yard his day off
sunning your prayers and his inability

to remember each word in its appropriate order

out the train window
this distortion becomes prominent
the man studies the face
of the boy behind his glasses
the woman reading her book

VI.

Preserved page of
whose young child
steps out contoured in blush
traces the lines of difficulty

                              ages unaltered
                              by true or false statements
                              categorized only
                              by degree of fear

if you substitute
the girl for yourself
the boy belongs somewhere
other than longing

                              for parades

in cold weather streets range in desolation

a boy clouds
the window with breath
of his desire to be
slow motioning
his development

         you hurry on, canceling all memories which pertain

in corners of doorways
he waits exactly as he is told
the word coming out
in specific anger

symptoms he has no control of

the time displayed
forever in quarter notes
on all-night radio stations
in rooms he is familiar with

he shares the thought
of train collision

levels of exhaustion
subside his father arrives
the moment dissolves into
3 years earlier

fences the height of
his hips not easily
climbed over

in streets of colder weather
the lost parade appears
hands in pockets

                              reach

for the designed passion
witnessed in love songs
or soft melodies which break

                              easily across the skin,
                              the bones absorb

in short sequences
our mothers dream
beyond our death
into fertile areas

                    gently falling
                    the sky fixes
                    sun a disappeared
                    hour rhythms of
                    disguised cycles

breathing becomes easily

the dance
in which
voices softer
are calling

                                        to this your voice

made up in colored
landscapes Europe
contains or Autumn
of October towns
loose in the impending
change of seasons

VII.

In dreams
gestures appear horrific
to the eyes of a young child
becomes an autobiography
in representation

                              a sequence
                              of told events
                              behind the voice
                              is the particular

disguise
as the boy loses his seat
on the train unfolds the map
to see which exit belongs
to him

research becomes
at length less of
a little girl
majority of a story
in pieces

                    a slow worker arrives back
at the train wreck, situation intact, seen climbing all over the cars,

                    the boy has his picture taken

you are persuaded to lose
this image leaves a gap
in history of any young child

goes back crying
home to his narrow
throat the sound is
contained

      a message becomes abstract outside the context

listening an isolated
movement towards control
remains futile

                we work late
                to terminate panic
                upheld promise toward
                the living thing in
                ourselves dying

        a newborn baby's death

            .

a cloud over the parade
people live in exile
of what they love
the camera motions for
us to smile

                as the clown passes
                his colors deepen
                in excitement you wave
                carry this incident
                towards the future
                relying on its clarity

        to motivate you

in order to be understood he talks in a voice other than
his own

as a sound blackens
the deeper inside a throat
it came from
upon entering cool air

dissuasion crowds
the slow worker
his eyes damaged
from return

VIII.

Snow in another part
of the country builds
in obstructions your
mother on her way home
cannot see

                        the baby towards entering death

flying west
for the boat ride
scattering of ashes
in the ocean Michael
row your boat ashore

           a trail of flowers and dust

                     you call with the words of begging
                     to any God figure to slow you down

place you into a photograph
of heat and vacation
where people are unaware

                     the boy in his pajamas
                     tiptoes to the edge of
                     the stairway listening to
                     the grief of others returns back
                     to the cold day

IX.

Pain of an eclipse in summer
following your birth kept under
glass heated for days your mother
sickening in her absence of you

                              the expanded season terminates itself
                              in waves of humidity dust returns
                              your name categorized beside small
                              footprints

interior secluded places one could be
                              crawled into

dreams interluding the 9 months
after conception, you or a christ figure
rising completes a cycle to be
celebrated by mass

                              the boy will be held onto
                              in time lapse photography
                              describes the birth with
                              a vocabulary of accident terms

immediate or crawl or rush or siren

a mother weeping
over lighted candles
on her way home from the
hospital the snow melts
you wait inside of
heated glass to be
brought away

in description you are becoming
older, the stars appear, when glimpsed at
from a distance, as white shadows
in a language supplying the necessary
communication for boys
this age

in his excitement
urinates the floor wet
with distilled bodily fluids
beautiful women
no longer beautiful

coming home one week later
as an infant you require less the
attention than you require now
only to be heat in the hot July weather

humidity the point of reconciliation
cute face of a baby
soft skin's arrival excites
the rest of the family

their hurried destination
being underprivileged people
who do not receive vacation days
inadequacy of the father returns to work

the skill of being born
in humidity allows a mother
to swim once she has fully recovered
in cooler weather we would not be
dreaming of boats

.

                              at the hardware store
                              the boy no longer waits on the sidewalk
                              for you to pass

but holds it all in

                              gets spoon fed for years
                              until you are old enough to hold the
                              fork or would be at the sight
                              of the wrecked train with stitches
                              in your foot being compared
                              to other boys your age

recognize events according to the degree of safety they offer avoid places which feel too smooth

well lighted or sufficient

> nurses take you
> from room to room
> adjusting the temperature
> of the hospital according
> to your degree of fever
> or chill

Catholic holidays
arrive too soon after
your birth
Parades in dark colors
disguised as soft events

.

your blood on my sheet
blends with the red linen
so that cloth cannot be distinguished
from liquid

X.

From several miles off
the coast
land appears sacred

        disturbing in its importance

he decorates his room
with portraits of a time
he felt equivalent to
the position of the world

           remembers himself exactly

       .

dozens occupy the train
going home from work
chronic thought of reproduction
dulls the senses of the young father
his name in vain upon the marquees
of nightclubs

The look of age during grief
causes the skin to roughen
added wrinkles on the palms

death of the baby
which will occur within those hours
that adjectives such as adorable
or charming
are being used
to describe your personality

sends you reeling toward any forgotten image
of being born

your sister wakes up
horrified by her missing
child/hood imagines the
boat ride to the island she
had never taken

in a distant room
her husband telephones
for arrangements detaching himself

from the scene in the photograph
where it was not necessary to plan for a funeral

XI.

Merge of symptoms
during the process
of rearrangement
relaying shocking news
to someone about to enter
the warm bath water
your body

                                        sweats in grieving
                                        the sensation of recreating
                                        an incident from the standpoint
                                        of a young body

feeling it exactly in your maturity, skin, hands, eyes, fingers

phosphates or colors of flesh
approaching the next country
you breathe more comfortably
when imagining your mother
holding you over the bathroom sink

anyone bearing a resemblance
to the notion of safety attracts
you swooning or the excitement of any boy

in his early teens

                                        religious holidays
                                        representing death
                                        in the form of beauty
                                        suffered died and was buried

in your mind the search
for prayer words
exhausts any other thought

coolness of a foreign country
in autumn confiscates
your fear holding onto someone
you love closely the road wet
from height of waves

having come too close
to the soft place in your heart
suddenly jerking myself away
you huddle, make plans for involvement
in a place more fragile

as your sister
after pain has been in her life
searching for tenderness
imagined the way her

brother's slow rowing towards shore in his silence

places we believe hold rest
roads covered with water from waves
off the island it takes almost
nine hours to reach land in the
storm as we unable to protect
each other re-experience being driven
home from school
with a stomach ache

vacations distort concepts
of emotion your father unable
to cry upon the news of death
later watches the boys
thought of bare history
his life in cycles

XII.

In an escape country
the tension mounts

from the surface
of one piece of land
can be seen the surface
of another

far off and disciplined
the boat approaches

XIII.

Afraid to hold
the stiff body of the baby
in the morgue the way tragedy
this silent portrayal
of disaster her purple lips
in death

                              exact nature of God
                              prayers inadequacy
                              empty from your hands
                              the white ash

of return

                    .

three months have passed
within a week photo
session of smiles you
contain finer moves
the insertion of jazz
your father recreates
places which he cannot
remember

                              a time before Christmas
                              and places would only last
                              as long as you could hold them

XIV.

Had the wreck occurred
4 years earlier you would not
have been watching with a
sense of confusion   went home
nightmaring
of being terrorized in the future

                                        the pain does not subside but with
                                        an acquitted quality disengages from
                                        impertinent situations

in colored places the dream recurring
remains black

four months simultaneously
after dying you dream the baby
is answering your questions
before she could talk
loving you holding with a look
in her eyes of remembering
places she had been
sounds she had made

insistence of feeling during the scatter of ashes out to sea

you lose track of time
Saturday evening go into
the sleeping sound of your
father's radio on all night
the baseball game

your mother working
through this emptiness
disbelieve the reassurance
of any mature voice in its attempts
to calm your direct terror of not even
a God figure to dream you out of dying
this gray sky, cool weather

.

At Oakland City Center 12th Street
several passengers seeing you crying
unaware of a train having derailed
in your young childhood

suffered, died and was buried
14 years ago the boy
in the hardware store tomorrow
will have lost interest in waiting
for you to arrive, go home early
pretending to be aloof

Paining him
the world and its relation
to having accurate perceptions
of feelings, desire

boys in the back car play
with the idea of sleeping alone
in the midst of diving
their gestures

incomplete

XV.

I could not bear
the thought of your mouth
touching another's yet in
my own inability persist
in the image of you her small hand or
face in the mirror

I occupy no space only to have
travelled a distance together
and gotten lost in a tragic place
where the slow drag of memory
intercepts Christmas

Desiring each other
in a mood or night bleached by
the full moon of the bath
words stop
movement resembles
waiting beyond our capability

descent of the boys
off high cliffs translucent
in shadows of your affair
mouth across somebody else's lips
I betray

In this time
of slow loss
verbal sounds only succeed
in displaying forms of terror

               having destroyed your belief
               in me to the point
               of dissuasion the slow worker
               reminisces of vacation days
               in which he will be able to
               sleep late or not pay attention

to words fixing themselves in the back of his mind

this experience remains distorted
in each of your eyes a father
unable to cry goes inside letting go of
the hand he is holding   faint surfacing of sounds
he recalls having heard

moments before he will witness the scene of his sister being killed

               in bed movements
               become strained
               adolescently I plan the party

without sensitivity of my betrayal
regarding your innocence
the baby's death resurfaces

see you on the street
close to the boy in the hardware store
finally his arms around you
shades of the sky resembling the photo
of my brother and I on the boat

in its slow movement toward the island

XVI.

Working late
to terminate panic
in the hardware store
the boy gestures
for you to follow him
inside tomorrow
being his day off
could hold you close

with a soft arm touching your skin, your stomach

                    provokes a challenge
                    the boys steady themselves
                    at the edge of the water
                    hesitating
                    until assured

their actions are not inappropriate

reorganize
the succession of events
having led up to the betrayal
black steam engines of trains
cars buckled into each other

.

On Easter
your sister crying
from the small girls in dresses
losing her child
airplanes above
near missing

        the bridge or below it
        children playing in refrigerator
        boxes from their lips a hollow memory
        steel and levers scraping against
        the metal tracks

in acts of betrayal location of silence

Michael rowing his boat
ashore the way Christ
will rise at Easter this year
and we will have felt
only a funeral

scattering of ashes out to sea your brother in his canoe
pretends to be silent

compassionate
for people who do not belong
the boy in the hardware store
makes himself feel welcome
by arriving on time 15 minutes
earlier

you will have been on your way home from the train wreck

scarcely believing
in voices below
crowded urgency
of a young baby's
hesitation
inside the blood
upon entering the room.

ACKNOWLEDGMENTS

Limited edition by San Francisco State University for Master of Arts in English: Creative Writing.

Copyright © 1988 by Lori Lubeski

ISBN: 0-929022-01-7

Library of Congress Catalogue Card Number: 88-090557

Other O Books

Phantom Anthems, Robert Grenier, 1986, $6.50
Dreaming Close By, Rick London, 1986, $5.00
Abjections: A Suite, Rick London, 1988, $3.50
Catenary Odes, Ted Pearson, 1987, $5.00
Visible Shivers, Tom Raworth, 1987, $8.00
O One/An Anthology, ed. Leslie Scalapino, 1988, $10.50
Return of the World, Todd Baron, 1988, $6.50
A Certain Slant of Sunlight, Ted Berrigan, 1988, $9.00

O Books
5729 Clover Drive
Oakland, CA 94618